W9-AXO-903

PARAMAHANSA YOGANANDA
(1893–1952)

HOW YOU CAN TALK *With* GOD

By

Paramahansa Yogananda

ABOUT THIS BOOK: *How You Can Talk With God* is compiled from two talks given by Paramahansa Yogananda in 1944 at the Self-Realization Fellowship temples he founded in San Diego and Hollywood, where it was his custom to speak on alternate Sundays. Often, after speaking on a certain topic at one temple, he would speak the following Sunday at the other, addressing different aspects of the same subject he had presented the previous week. His talks through the years were taken down stenographically by one of his earliest and closest disciples, Sri Daya Mata (president and spiritual head of Self-Realization Fellowship since 1955). *How You Can Talk With God* was first published in 1957, and has been translated into French, German, Italian, Portuguese, and Spanish.

Authorized by the International Publications Council of
SELF-REALIZATION FELLOWSHIP
3880 San Rafael Avenue
Los Angeles, California 90065-3298

First hardcover printing, 1998

ISBN 0-87612-168-7
Printed in the United States of America
12629-54321

The glory of God is great. He is real, and He can be found.... Silently and surely, as you walk on the path of life, you must come to the realization that God is the only object, the only goal that will satisfy you; for in God lies the answer to every desire of the heart.

—Paramahansa Yogananda

HOW YOU CAN TALK *With* GOD

Talking with God is a definite fact. In India I have been in the presence of saints while they were talking with the Heavenly Father. And all of you, also, may communicate with Him; not a one-sided conversation, but a real talk wherein you speak to God and He responds. Everyone can talk *to* the Lord, of course. But I am discussing today how we may persuade Him to reply to us.

Why should we doubt? The scriptures of the world abound in descriptions of talks between God and man. One of the most beautiful of these incidents is recorded in I Kings 3:5–13 in the Bible: "The Lord appeared to Solomon in a dream by night; and God said, Ask what I shall give thee. And Solomon said.…Give therefore Thy servant an understanding heart.…And God said unto him, Because thou hast asked this thing, and hast not asked for thyself long life; neither hast asked riches for thyself, nor hast asked the life of thine enemies; but hast asked for thyself understanding to discern judgment; Behold, I have done according to thy words: lo, I have given thee a wise and an understanding heart…And I have also given thee that which thou hast not asked, both riches and honor."

David, too, held converse many times with the Lord, and discussed even mundane matters with Him. "And David inquired of God, saying, Shall I go up against the Philistines? and wilt Thou deliver them into mine hand? And the Lord said unto him, Go up; for I will deliver them into thine hand."*

God Is Moved Only by Love

The average man prays to God with his mind only, not with all the fervor of his heart.

* I Chronicles 14:10.

Such prayers are too weak to bring any response. We should speak to the Divine Spirit with confidence and with a feeling of closeness, as to a father or a mother. Our relationship with God should be one of unconditional love. More than in any other relationship we may rightfully and naturally demand a reply from Spirit in Its aspect as the Divine Mother. God is constrained to answer such an appeal; for the essence of a mother is love and forgiveness of her child, no matter how great a sinner he may be. The relationship between mother and child is the most beautiful form of human love that the Lord has given us.

A definite conception of God (such as that of the Divine Mother) is necessary, otherwise one does not receive a clear response. And the demand for the Lord's reply should be strong; a half-believing prayer is not sufficient. If you make up your mind: "He *is* going to talk with me"; if you refuse to believe differently, regardless of how many years He has not answered you; if you go on trusting Him, one day He will respond.

I have written in *Autobiography of a Yogi* about some of the numerous occasions on which I have talked with God. My first experience in hearing the Divine Voice came when I was a little child. Sitting on my bed one morning, I fell into a deep reverie.

"What is behind the darkness of closed

eyes?" This probing thought came powerfully into my mind. An immense flash of light at once manifested to my inner gaze. Divine shapes of saints, sitting in meditation in mountain caves, formed like miniature cinema pictures on the large screen of radiance within my forehead.

"Who are you?" I spoke aloud.

"We are the Himalayan yogis." The celestial response is difficult to describe; my heart was thrilled. The vision vanished, but the silvery beams expanded in ever widening circles to infinity.

I said, "What is this wondrous glow?"

"I am Ishwara (the Lord). I am Light." The Voice was as murmuring clouds.

My mother and eldest sister Roma were nearby when I had this early experience, and they too heard the Divine Voice. I received such happiness from God's response that I determined then and there to search for Him until I would become wholly one with Him.

Most people think there is only darkness behind closed eyes. But, as you develop spiritually and concentrate on the "single" eye in the forehead, you will find that your inner sight is opened. You will behold another world, one of many lights and great beauty. Visions of saints, such as those I saw of

Himalayan yogis, will appear before you. If your concentration goes still deeper, you too will hear the Voice of God.

Again and again the scriptures tell us of the Lord's promise that He will communicate with us. "And ye shall seek Me, and find Me, when ye shall search for Me with all your heart."—Jeremiah 29:13. "The Lord is with you, while ye be with Him; and if ye seek Him, He will be found of you; but if ye forsake Him, He will forsake you."—II Chronicles 15:2. "Behold, I stand at the door, and knock: if any man hear My voice, and open the door, I will come in to him, and will sup with him, and he with Me."—Revelation 3:20.

If you can just once "break bread" with the Lord, break His silence, He will talk often with you. But in the beginning it is very difficult; it is not easy to become acquainted with God, because He wants to be sure that you really desire to know Him. He gives tests to see if the devotee wants Him or something else. He will not talk with you until you have convinced Him that no other desire is hiding in your heart. Why should He reveal Himself to you if your heart is filled only with longings for His gifts?

Man's Love Is His Sole Gift to God

The whole creation was designed as a test for man. By our conduct in this world we disclose whether we want the Lord or His gifts. God will not tell you that you should desire Him above all else, because He wants your love to be freely given, without "prompting." That is the whole secret in the game of this universe. He who created us yearns for our love. He wants us to give it spontaneously, without His asking. Our love is the one thing God does not possess, unless we choose to bestow it. So, you see, even the Lord has something to attain: our love. And we shall never be happy until we give it. So long as we are wayward children, pygmies crawling on this ball of earth and crying for His gifts while we ignore Him, the Giver, we fall into many pits of misery.

As God is the Essence of our own being, we cannot truly express ourselves until we learn to manifest His presence within us. This is the truth. It is because we are Divine, a part of Him, that we are unable to find lasting satisfaction in anything material. "Naught shelters thee, who wilt not shelter Me."* Until you attain contentment in God, you will not win contentment from anything else.

* *The Hound of Heaven,* by Francis Thompson.

Is God Personal or Impersonal?

Is God personal or impersonal? A little discussion of this point will help you in your attempts to communicate with Him. Many people don't like to think of the Lord as personal; they feel that an anthropomorphic conception is limiting. They consider Him to be Impersonal Spirit, All-Power, the Intelligent Force that is responsible for the universe.

But if our Creator is impersonal, how is it that He has created human beings? We are personal; we have individuality. We think, feel, will; and God has given us not only the power to appreciate the thoughts and feelings of others but to respond to them. The Lord is surely not devoid of the spirit of reciprocity that animates His own creatures. When we permit it, our Heavenly Father can and will establish a personal relationship with each one of us.

Considering the impersonal aspect of God, we get the impression of a Remote Being, One who merely receives the prayer-thoughts we offer, without responding to them; One who knows everything, yet maintains a heartless silence. But this is a philosophical error, because God is everything: personal as well as impersonal. He created persons, human beings. Their Originator could not be wholly impersonal.

It satisfies a deep need in our hearts to

think that God may take a human form and come to us and talk with us. Why doesn't He do it for everyone? Many saints have heard the voice of God. Why can't you? "Thou, O Lord, art invisible, impersonal, unknown, and unknowable; yet I believe that by my devotion's frost, Thou canst be 'frozen' into a form." God can be persuaded to take a personal form by your intense devotion. You, like St. Francis of Assisi and other great ones, may see the living body of Christ, if you pray deeply enough. Jesus was a personal manifestation of God. He who knows Brahma (God) is Brahma himself. Did not Christ say: "I and my Father are one"?* Swami Shankara also

* John 10:30.

declared: "I am Spirit" and "Thou art That." We have the word of many great prophets that all men are made in the image of Divinity.

I receive much of my knowledge from God, rather than from books. I seldom read. I tell you what I have perceived directly. That is why I speak with authority, the authority of my direct perception of Truth. The opinion of the whole world may stand against it, but the authority of direct perception will always be accepted eventually.

Meaning of "The Image of God"

In the Bible we read: "For in the image of God made He man."* No one has ever fully explained in what ways man is the image of God. God is Spirit; and man, in his essential nature, is also Spirit. That is the primary meaning of the Biblical passage, but there are many other true interpretations as well.

The whole human body and the consciousness and motion in it are a microcosmic representation of God. In consciousness is omniscience and omnipresence. You can immediately think you are at the North Star or on

* Genesis 9:6

Mars. In thought there is no gulf between you and anything else. By virtue of the consciousness within man, therefore, he may be said to be made in the image of God.

Consciousness is aware of itself; it intuitively feels itself. God, through His cosmic consciousness, is aware of Himself in every atom of creation. "Are not two sparrows sold for a farthing? and one of them shall not fall on the ground without [the awareness of] your Father."*

Man also has the innate power of cosmic consciousness, though few develop it. Man also has will, whereby he, like the Creator, can

* Matthew 10:29

create worlds instantaneously; but few develop that power which is within them. The animals cannot reason, but man can. All the attributes that God has—consciousness, reason, will, feeling, love—man has too. In these qualities man may be said to be made in the image of God.

The Physical Body Is Not Matter, but Energy

The energy that we feel in the body implies the existence of a vaster power than is required just to operate the individual physical vehicle. The power of cosmic energy that sustains universes is vibrating in our bodies also. Cosmic energy is one aspect of God. Therefore we are made in His image even from the physical standpoint.

What is the energy we have in the body? Our physical form is made of molecules, molecules are made of atoms, atoms are made of electrons, and electrons are made of life force or "lifetrons"—countless billions of specks of energy. With your spiritual eye you can see the body as a mass of scintillating specks of light—the energy that is emanating from your twenty-seven thousand billion cells. Only through delusion do you see the body as solid flesh. In reality it is not matter, but energy.

It is because you think you are made of flesh

and blood that you sometimes imagine yourself to be a weakling. But if you register the consciousness of God in your body, you will realize that flesh is nothing more than a physical manifestation of the five vibratory elements of earth, water, fire, air, and ether.

Five Universal Elements Compose Man's Body

The whole universe—which is God's body—is made of the same five elements that compose man's body. The starlike shape of the human body represents the rays of these five elements. The head, the two hands, and the two feet form the five points of the star. So in this way, too, we are made in the image of God.

The five fingers also represent the five vibratory elements of the Cosmic Intelligent Vibration that maintain the structure of creation. The thumb represents the grossest vibratory element, earth; hence its thickness. The first finger represents the water element. The second finger represents the darting fire element; that is why it is the longest. The third finger represents air. The smallest finger represents ether, which is very fine.

Rubbing each finger animates the particular power that it represents. Hence rubbing the middle finger (representing the fire element) and the navel (opposite the lumbar or "fire" center in the spine, which governs digestion and assimilation) will help one to overcome indigestion.

God manifests motion in creation. Man has developed legs and feet because of the urge to express motion. The toes are materializations of the five rays of energy.

The eyes epitomize God the Father, Son, and Holy Ghost in the pupil, iris, and white. When you concentrate at the point between the eyebrows, the current in the two eyes reflects as one light, and you behold the spiritual eye. This single orb is the "eye of God." We have developed two eyes because of the law of relativity that prevails in our dualistic universe. Jesus said, "If therefore thine eye be single, thy whole body shall be full of light."* If we look through the spiritual eye, the single eye of God, we perceive that all creation is made of one substance, His light.

One With God, One With God's Power

In the ultimate sense man has all power. You can change anything you want to when your consciousness is united with God's. Automobile parts can be replaced or changed, as needful; but to effect a similar change in

* Matthew 6:22.

the physical body is more complicated. Mind, which controls all the cells, is the basic factor. When a man attains full control of mind, his bodily cells and parts may be replaced or changed as often as desired, and at will. For example, he could, just by a thought, cause the bodily atoms to change and bring into being a whole new set of teeth. There is complete control of matter when one is advanced spiritually.

The Lord is Spirit; the Impersonal is invisible. But when He created the physical world He became God the Father. As soon as He assumed the role of Creator, He became personal. He became visible: this whole universe is the body of God.

In the form of the earth He has a positive and a negative side—the north and south poles. The stars are His eyes, the grass and trees are His hair, and the rivers are His bloodstream. The ocean's roar, the skylark's song, the cry of the newborn babe, and all other sounds of creation are His voice. This is the personal God. The heartthrob behind all hearts is His pulsing cosmic energy. He is walking in mankind's twenty-six hundred million pairs of feet. He is working through all hands. It is the One Divine Consciousness that is manifesting through all brains.

Because of God's law of attraction and repulsion, the cells of the human body are harmoniously held together in the same way that stars are kept in balance in their proper orbits. The omnipresent Lord is ever active; there is not a place anywhere without some form of life. With illimitable prodigality God incessantly projects protean forms—inexhaustible manifestations of His cosmic energy.

The Divine Spirit had a specific idea or pattern in mind when He created. He first externalized the whole universe, then created man. In forming for Himself a physical body of planetary systems, God manifested three aspects: cosmic consciousness, cosmic energy, and cosmic mass or matter.

These three correspond respectively to man's ideational or causal body, astral or energy body, and physical body. And the soul or Life behind them is Spirit.

Spirit manifests macrocosmically as cosmic consciousness, cosmic energy, and the body of universes; and microcosmically as human consciousness, human energy, and the human body. Again we see that man has indeed been made in the Divine Image.

God "Talks" Through Vibration

God *does* appear to us in physical form. He is more personal than you can imagine. He is as real and actual as you are. This is what I want

By Jagannath (Kalyana-Kalpataru)

THE DIVINE MOTHER

God in the aspect of Divine Mother is represented in Hindu art as a four-armed woman. One hand is upraised, signifying universal blessing; in the other three hands she holds prayer beads, representing devotion; pages of scripture, symbolizing learning and wisdom; and an artistic jar, representing wealth.

to tell you today. The Lord is ever responding to us. The vibration of His thought is constantly being sent forth; this requires energy; the energy manifests as sound. There is a very strong point here. God is consciousness. God is energy. "Talking" means vibrating. In the vibration of His cosmic energy He is talking all the time. He has become the Mother of creation that materializes Herself as solids, liquids, fire, air, and ether.

The invisible Mother is continuously expressing Herself in terms of visible forms—in flowers, mountains, seas, and stars. What is matter? Nothing but a particular rate of vibration of God's cosmic energy. No form in the universe is really solid. That which appears so is merely a compact or gross vibration of His energy. The Lord is talking to us through vibrations. But the question is, how to communicate directly with Him? That is the most difficult accomplishment of all: to talk with God.

If you speak to a mountain, it doesn't answer. Talk to the flowers, as Luther Burbank did, and you may feel in them a little response. And of course we can talk to other people. But is God less responsive than flowers and human beings, that He lets us keep on talking to Him and yet fails to answer us? It appears that way, doesn't it? The trouble is not with Him, but with us. Our intuitive telephonic system is out of order. God is calling us and speaking to us, but we do not hear Him.

Cosmic Vibration "Speaks" All Languages

But saints hear Him. Whenever a certain master I knew would pray, God's answering voice would seem to come from the sky. God doesn't need a throat in order to speak. If you pray strongly enough, those prayer vibrations bring a vibratory response immediately. It manifests in whatever language you are accustomed to hearing. If you are praying in German you hear the reply in German. If you talk in English you hear the answer in English.

The vibrations of different languages originate in the cosmic vibration. God, being the cosmic vibration, knows all languages. What is language? It is a certain vibration. What is vibration? It is a certain energy. And what is energy? It is a certain thought.

Though God hears all our prayers He does not always respond. Our situation is like that of a child who calls for his mother, but the mother does not think it necessary to come. She sends him a plaything to keep him quiet. But when the child refuses to be comforted by anything except the mother's presence, she comes. If you want to know God, you must be like the naughty baby who cries till the mother comes.

If you make up your mind never to stop

crying for Her, Divine Mother will talk with you. No matter how busy She is with Her housework of creation, if you persist in your cries, She is bound to speak. The Hindu scriptures tell us that if for one night and one day, without a moment's interruption, a devotee talks to God with intense devotion, He will respond. But how few will do it! Every day you have "important engagements"—the "devil" that keeps you away from God. The Lord will not come if you just say a little prayer and then start thinking of something else; or if you pray like this: "Heavenly Father, I am calling to You, but I am awfully sleepy. Amen." St. Paul said, "Pray without ceasing."*

* I Thessalonians 5:17.

Patient Job held long conversations with God. Job said to Him: "Hear, I beseech Thee, and I will speak. I will demand of Thee; and declare Thou unto me. I have heard of Thee by the hearing of the ear; but now mine eye seeth Thee."*

When a lover protests his devotion mechanically, his beloved knows that his words are not sincere; she is "hearing" what is really in his heart. Similarly, when God's devotees pray to Him He knows whether their hearts and minds are dry of devotion and whether their thoughts are dashing wildly everywhere; He does not respond to halfhearted calls. But to those devotees who day and night with

* Job 42:4–5.

utmost intensity pray and talk to Him, He does appear. To such devotees He comes without fail.

Do Not Be Satisfied With Less Than the Highest

Don't waste time in seeking little things. Naturally it is easier to get other gifts from God than the supreme gift of Himself. But don't be satisfied with anything less than the highest. I haven't cared about the gifts that have come to me from God, except that I see, behind them, Him who is the Giver. Why are all my desires materialized? Because I go deep; I go straight to God. In every aspect of creation

I see Him. He is our Father; He is nearer than the nearest, dearer than the dearest, more real than anybody else. He is both unknowable and knowable.

God is crying for you. He wants you to return to Him. It is your birthright. You will have to leave this earth someday; it is not an abiding-place for you. Earth life is only a school in which He has put us to see how we shall behave here; that is all. Before He will reveal Himself God wants to know whether we desire earth's tinsel glory or whether we have acquired enough wisdom to say:

"I am through with all this, Lord. I want to talk with You alone. I know You are all I really own. You will be with me when everyone else is gone."

Human beings are seeking happiness in marriage, in money, in wine, and so forth; but such people are puppets of destiny. Once this realization is attained, one finds out the true purpose of life and naturally begins to seek God.

We must claim our lost divine heritage. The more unselfish one is, the more he tries to give happiness to others, the more likely he will be to think about God. And the more one thinks of worldly goals and of human desires, the farther his soul's happiness recedes from him. We were not put here on earth to grovel in the mud of the senses and get nipped with sufferings at every turn. That which is of the world is evil because it suppresses the bliss of the soul. The greatest happiness comes by immersing the mind in thoughts of God.

Why Postpone Happiness?

Why don't you think ahead? Why do you consider nonessentials so important? Most people concentrate on breakfast, lunch, and dinner, work, social activities, and so on. Make your life more simple and put your whole mind on the Lord. Earth is a place of preparation for getting back to God. He wants to see if we love Him more than His gifts. He is the

Father and all of us are His children. He has a right to our love and we have a right to His love. Our troubles arise because we neglect Him. But He is always waiting.

I only wish He had put a little more sense in all of us. We have the freedom to cast God away or to accept Him. And here we are begging, begging, begging for a little money, a little happiness, a little love. Why ask for things that must be taken away from you one day? How long shall you be moaning about money and sickness and difficulties? Seize immortality and the kingdom of God! That is what you really want.

A Divine Kingdom Is at Stake

The saints stress nonattachment so that one strong point of material attachment may not prevent our attaining the entire kingdom of God. Renunciation doesn't mean giving up everything; it means giving up small pleasures for eternal bliss. God talks to you when you are working for Him, and you should speak to Him constantly. Tell Him any thought that comes into your mind. And say to Him, "Lord, reveal Thyself, reveal Thyself." Don't take silence for an answer. He will first respond by giving you something that you have wanted, showing you that you are in His attention. But don't be content with His gifts. Let Him know that you will never be satisfied until you have Him. Finally He will give you an answer. In a vision you may see a face of some saintly being, or you may hear a Divine Voice talking to you; and you will know that you are in communion with God.

To coax Him to give Himself takes steady, unceasing zeal. Nobody can teach you that zeal. You have to develop that yourself. "You can take a horse to water but you cannot make him drink." Yet when the horse is thirsty it seeks out water with zeal. So, when you have an immense thirst for the Divine, when you will not give undue importance to anything else—the tests of the world or the tests of the body—then He will come. Remember, when your heart-call is intense, when you accept no excuse, then He will come.

You must remove from your mind all doubt that God will answer. Most people don't get any response because of their disbelief. If you are absolutely determined that you are going to attain something, nothing can stop you. It is when you give up that you write the verdict against yourself. The man of success doesn't know the word "impossible."

Faith is the limitless power of God within you. God knows through His consciousness that He created everything; so faith means knowledge and conviction that we are made in the image of God. When we are attuned to His consciousness within us, we can create worlds. Remember, in your will lies the almighty power of God. When a host of difficulties comes and you refuse to give up in spite of them; when your mind becomes "set," then you will find God responding to you.

God, being cosmic vibration, is the Word. God as the Word is humming through all atoms. There is a music coming out of the universe that deeply meditating devotees can hear. Now, at this moment, I am hearing His voice. The Cosmic Sound* that you hear in meditation is the voice of God. That sound forms

* *Aum (Om),* the conscious, intelligent, cosmic vibration or Holy Ghost.

itself into language intelligible to you. When I listen to *Aum* and occasionally ask God to tell me something, that sound of *Aum* changes into English or Bengali language and gives me precise instructions.

God also talks to man through his intuition. If you learn how to listen* to the Cosmic Vibration it is easier to hear His voice. But even if you just pray to God through the cosmic ether, if your will is strong enough the ether will respond with His voice. He is ever talking to you, saying:

"Call Me, speak unto Me from the depths

* Through a certain ancient technique taught in *Self-Realization Fellowship Lessons.*

of your heart, from the core of your being, from the very depths of your soul, persistently, majestically, determinedly, with a firm resolve in your heart that you will go on seeking Me, no matter how many times I do not answer. If you unceasingly whisper in your heart to Me, 'O my silent Beloved, speak to me,' I will come to you, My devotee."

If once you can get that response you will never feel separated from Him again. The divine experience will always remain with you. But that "once" is difficult because the heart and mind are not convinced; doubt creeps in because of our previous materialistic beliefs.

God Answers the Heart Whispers of True Devotees

God will answer every human being, irrespective of caste, creed, or color. There is a saying in Bengali that if you give a soul call to God as the Universal Mother, She cannot remain silent. She has to speak. That is beautiful, isn't it?

Think of all the things that came to me today and that I have told you. You should never again doubt that God will respond to you, if you are constant and persistent in your demands. "And the Lord spake unto Moses face to face, as a man speaketh unto his friend."*

* Exodus 33:11.

About the Author

Paramahansa Yogananda (1893–1952) is widely regarded as one of the preeminent spiritual figures of our time. Born in northern India, he came to the United States in 1920, where for more than thirty years he taught India's ancient science of meditation and the art of balanced spiritual living. Through his acclaimed life story, *Autobiography of a Yogi,* and his numerous other books, Paramahansa Yogananda has introduced millions of readers to the perennial wisdom of the East. Under the guidance of one of his earliest and closest disciples, Sri Daya Mata, his spiritual and humanitarian work is carried on by Self-Realization Fellowship, the international society he founded in 1920 to disseminate his teachings worldwide.

Also by Paramahansa Yogananda

Available at bookstores or directly from the publisher:

Self-Realization Fellowship
3880 San Rafael Avenue • Los Angeles, California 90065
Tel (213) 225-2471 • Fax (213) 225-5088
www.yogananda-srf.org

Autobiography of a Yogi

In the Sanctuary of the Soul: *A Guide To Effective Prayer*

Where There Is Light: *Insight and Inspiration for Meeting Life's Challenges*

The Law of Success

Metaphysical Meditations

Scientific Healing Affirmations

The Science of Religion

Man's Eternal Quest

The Divine Romance

Journey to Self-Realization: *Discovering the Gifts of the Soul*

God Talks With Arjuna: *The Bhagavad Gita—A New Translation and Commentary*

Wine of the Mystic: *The Rubaiyat of Omar Khayyam—A Spiritual Interpretation*

Whispers from Eternity

Sayings of Paramahansa Yogananda

Songs of the Soul

Cosmic Chants